Life Changes:

A BOOMER'S JOURNEY

Michael G. Upchurch

Copyright© 2025 by Michael G. Upchurch

All Rights Reserved

No part of this book may be reproduced or transmitted
in any form or by any means, electronic or mechanical,
including photocopying, recording, or by any
information storage and retrieval system without the
written permission of the author, except where
permitted by law.

First edition 2025

To all those boomers who have made it through trying years and can now look back to those good and bad times.

Acknowledgments

I would like to recognize those who have kindly "put up with me" in this endeavor. In particular to my cousin, Johnny Lacy. J. K. Spivey, Amberly Henderson, and to my lovely wife, Beverley, who supported me in this endeavor. Also, I would like to recognize Amazon Publishing for having the patience with me as I navigated these uncharted waters.

Table of Contents

Foreword

I have, for many years, toyed with the thought of writing a book. Early on, I envisioned smoking a pipe on the front porch of a mountain cabin with the aroma of the fireplace burning while writing my book. Things have changed since then. I am much older, I don't smoke anymore, and I haven't been back to that cabin since. Now that I have finally decided to sit down and start my book, I have found myself trying to decide on the most appropriate genre for the book. Three authors whom I admire are Lewis Grizzard, Erma Bambeck, and Jeanne Robinson, as their styles fit more appropriately with how I view my life experiences. Life is full of good and bad experiences. I captured this in the story "You Meet the Strangest People at a Bar."

Since I started writing this book, a lot of my acquaintances/friends have wanted to know if I was going to include them. The short answer is possibly, or I've got to think about it. All this attention to their possible notoriety got me thinking about who I should include. This quickly reminded me of a friend with whom I worked. One day, we got into a discussion about the difference between a friend and an acquaintance. The conversation was intense, with opposing viewpoints. I would call this an HDR (heavy, deep, and real).

Back to the topic, this friend's definition was unique and to the point. He stated that he had five individuals whom he considered friends and had many acquaintances. His definition of an acquaintance was one that you called in the middle of the night asking them to come and give you a ride home. Your acquaintance would respond by stating that they have a few things to take care of and to just stay with the car until they arrive. The friend would state that they are out the door to come pick you up. I find this definition to be straightforward and honest, in strict terms, "I got your back."

This brings up my philosophy on the types of people that I meet. I call them "Zebras". As you know, zebras have both "white" and "black" stripes. Nothing unique. However, I think this fits my definition. Think about it, "white" and 'black" stripes; "yes" and "no," "liberal" and "conservative." You name it, most of the examples fall into these two categories. Do they not?

Let me explain. There is a transition between the "white" and 'black" stripes, a blend of the two colors, "Shades of Grey." As you might surmise, these are individuals who can see both sides of a predicament and the benefits of each position, and there are examples abound to support this position. I must admit I'm in the "Shades of Grey" camp. I passionately believe that if all of humanity would stop and listen, we could solve a lot of our differences.

Recently, while I was at a bar/grill having my beverage, I was looking at the other patrons and wondering what their lives were like. Everybody has a story, some good and some bad, some interesting and some boring.

I tried to capture both my good times and bad times but in a light, hardy mood. It spans a time from when, as a boy, my values were formed, to my teenage years, when I realized that I wasn't too smart in my early years. I guess the same could apply to my current life.

I have tried to document my life positions and beliefs in this book. I have built my career upon "quality." This is noted in the description of the navy and my various jobs. I firmly believe in validating events, conversations, and documentation. I hope you enjoy traveling back to the time when we were young and naive, to the later years in life when one is still naive.

Furthermore, I have made every attempt to give due credit where possible.

Early Years

Life Growing up in the '60s

My early years were nothing fantastic. I did the typical "stupid stuff." We lived on Marion Circle in Decatur, Georgia, which does not add anything to the story. That aside, I remember one Christmas when I got a Lionel train set and a BB rifle gun.

My mother had me sit on a department store Santa's knee and have that "cheesy" picture made. Man, did I look like a "dork," which carried forward into my early years? Of course, the department store Santa told me he would bring both items to me on Christmas morning … he did! When I got up, I immediately found my Red Rider BB gun lying under the Christmas tree. Later that morning, my enthusiasm was quickly dampened when I was playing with my Red Rider BB gun and shooting at who "knows what," and I broke a window in the house across the street. Yep, the BB gun was then sent to the "vault" known as my "parents' room." I never saw that BB gun again. It took two more years before I realized that Santa was not real ... so much for the "cheesy" pictures.

As an imaginative kid, I did the typical "stupid stuff," such as playing army by throwing eggs at anything and everything. Just like a John Wayne war movie, I figured out that eggs, when thrown against a front door, looked and sounded just like a hand grenade exploding. So, what do you think I did? I threw eggs at the neighbor's front doors, and just like I thought when they "hit the door" with a resounding "splat." I was so thrilled. This went on for about a week when the neighbors complained to my mother that the busted eggs didn't come off their front door.

I vaguely remember Mother complaining about the missing eggs. At my young age, I could never figure out how she knew about the missing eggs. She also must have eyes in the back of her head. Mother rode that "horse" until it died.

As nice as she was, mother had a temper to match. She always told me that she got that from my grandmother. This explanation seemed appropriate since her maiden name was Cain. My grandmother would always say my mother was "raising cane." The story goes that my mother was a handful when she was five or six years old. Grandmother got tired of trying to find my mother, so she took her to the bedroom and made her sit down on the floor next to the bed. Grandmother then picked up the bedpost and set it down on my mother's dress, along with the admonishment not to tear her dress. If she did, my grandmother would tell my grandfather, who was a stern disciplinarian. According to my mother, Granddaddy had a mean swing with a belt. One that any baseball player would dream of having.

Daytona Beach, Florida

Fast forward a few years to our summer vacations. Mother wanted to make sure that we had a vacation during the summer school break. These trips were always to Daytona Beach, Florida. Mother would volunteer to take three of my cousins along with my brother and me. Now, taking five rambunctious kids of 6 to 10 years old, one would have to be brave. On one of these trips, one of my cousins and I got into a 'pissing" match. Mother told us to quit, and we didn't, so the next time we started up, she took aim and proceeded to smack us. I never knew that she could pack such a wallop. The only thing I can think of is that when she was young, she would've been on the receiving end of one of those round house swings.

Nowadays, the disciplinary measures used back then would be considered abuse. However, I still remember my mother's swing. Mother was not bashful about pulling the car over to the side of the road, getting us out of the car, and spanking us. She could have been submitted for an award for her spanking technique. She would grab our left arm with her right arm and proceed to spank us unruly kids. I looked like a merry-go-round, trying to avoid that baseball swing on my rear. There I was, jumping and screaming, promising never to do the bad thing again, whatever it was.

This was the same trip where I found a seashell that I wanted to take home. Another lesson learned... be sure to check that there are no residents in the seashell. I kept the seashell and its occupant in a jar of seawater. After a couple of days in the warm summer sun, the resident, who was a small octopus, promptly died. The motel management asked my mother to leave early because a dead octopus in a glass jar, which smells very potent, is bad for business. I mean, how would you like to go to the pool if the only smell is a dead octopus? Again, another lesson learned ... then there was my mother's brother, Uncle Fred. He and my mother shared the same disciplinary upbringing. My cousin was constantly backtalking to my uncle. Same scenario, stopping on the roadside, providing the mandatory punishment with a stem warning not to open his mouth until they arrived at their destination. A few hours later, as they were getting out of the car, Uncle Fred noticed that one of my cousin's shoes was missing. The obvious question was, "Where is your other shoe?"

"I lost it back on the side of the road where you spanked me."

A frustrated Uncle Fred wanted to know why my cousin didn't tell him about the missing shoe; my cousin's answer was simple, "Well, Dad, you told me not to open my mouth until we got to our destination." After additional hours of driving back for the shoe, it was returned to its rightful owner.

As Paul Harvey would say, "and the rest of the story…"

Yeah, I wonder if my cousin received any punishment … probably so.

Religious Upbringing and Puberty

During these formative years, my grandmother decided that my brother and I needed more of a religious upbringing. This was a sore point for my grandparents since my parents were not avid churchgoers. My grandparents would come to our house and take my brother and me to church on Sunday. Since my grandparents were practicing Catholics, that's where we attended church. Eventually, my parents gave in to my grandparents and agreed that it would be a good idea for me to do my 6th and 7th grades at a church parochial school.

This would give me some well-needed discipline and, hopefully, some religion.

The only thing I got was a lot of corporal punishment from the teacher, who just happened to be a Catholic nun. No, they did not look like those in the movie *Change of Habit* or the *Flying Nun*. They could be circus "hawker" on a street corner "barking" the virtues of discipline. "Come over and see the type of discipline we have for you," I mentioned my parents and grandparents being stern disciplinarians, but they did not come close to what I received in parochial school.

My early years of making it through puberty with no mental scars were short-lived when my father had to tell me about the "birds and bees." The question that I have is why did they call it the "birds and bees?" We don't make babies like they do. Can you imagine the quandary I was in trying to reconcile in my mind how they made babies? Thank goodness my brother gave me the facts. I can say that all he told me was that a baby is inside a woman, and then one day, when you wake up and "bata-boom," there's the baby.

What a waste of my time. Birds and bees aside, my early life growing up was a lot like the TV sitcom series *"Leave It to Beaver."* I don't want to leave you in the dark. It was a black-and-white sitcom on TV that tried to duplicate everyday life back in the late 50s and early 60s. The dad would come home from work, remove his coat, and then sit in the living room chair smoking a pipe and reading the newspaper dispensing fatherly advice while the mom was in the kitchen preparing dinner. (They ALWAYS ate dinner at 5 pm). She was dressed up in an apron and high heel shoes, making dinner. Since both of my parents worked long hours, I learned a lot about the right and wrong things to do in life from this TV series. The philosophy was practical and straightforward. It became the framework for a solid foundation to guide me to be a typical "good kid."

Peg Leg Pete

One of my earliest memories with my grandparents was spending a week with them in the summertime. Every summer, I would spend time "in the country" with my grandparents. Those summers left many memories of my childhood, that is, those that I can still remember at a later age. After my parents left me there for the summer vacation, my grandfather would lay down the various rules I had to follow. Of course, I never listened. ('In one ear and out the other' as my grandfather would say.)

Oh well, I have numerous memories centered around days when I would help with the garden, sitting on the front porch listening to tales of unexplained events. But most of all, there are three events that stand out in my memory of that time in my life: having an "outhouse" with a Sears and Roebuck catalog, chewing tobacco, and raising chickens.

These were the days of country dirt roads, water wells, and outdoor plumbing (outhouse). This "facility," which is a nice way to describe it, was not close to the house because of the obvious odor, which was mighty strong in the summertime. Additionally, this" facility" gave rise to the "satellite facility" under the bed in the house, known as the porcelain pot for emergency needs during the night. Now, if you are an individual who likes to read while doing your "constitution," a "Sears and Roebuck catalog" is provided for enlightenment during your visit. Those who do not know what a "Sears and Roebuck catalog" is should think of it as an Amazon in print form. Just imagine going through page after page, looking for a special item. As a side note, you forgot to bring the toilet paper with you; just use a few pages from the catalog ... yuk! This reminds me of another memory that I can never forget, and that was my first time chewing tobacco.

Now, my grandmother was against tobacco of any kind: cigars, cigarettes, corn cob pipes, snuff, and chewing tobacco. I think the main reason she was against tobacco was that when my grandfather chewed, he was constantly spitting and had horrendous bad breath, and yes, he sometimes had a little drool down the side of his mouth.

He chewed a special brand called "Bull of

the Woods" (Yeah, I'm not sure why it was named as such because if you were not used to it, you were not a "bull"). Because he knew my grandmother's disdain for tobacco, he was particular about spitting out the tobacco and rinsing out his mouth before he entered the house. Oh, I wanted to be like my grandfather, so I decided that I would try his chewing tobacco. This tobacco was about the size and texture of an over cooked chocolate brownie. Back then, they didn't think it was necessary to put the "Best if Used By date" on the wrapper. Of course, back then, chewing tobacco would not go bad. In fact, you could not determine if it was still good or not. Well, wanting to be like my grandfather, one day, when he was not around, I bit off a good-sized bite of his chewing tobacco, also known as a "plug" in those days. I was so proud to be like my grandfather, chewing tobacco for at least 30 minutes. Then, I started turning green, dizzy, and nauseous. As you can surmise, I didn't fare well. Nowhere on the packaging did it say not to swallow the juice but rather to spit it out. When I went to the house complaining about not feeling well to my grandmother, she took one look at me and knew exactly what I was doing. She could tell I had been into Grandpa's chewing tobacco by the big wad of tobacco that made my cheek poke out. Oh, and the juice that I refused to spit out. I already knew what would happen to my well-being when I "turned green" and became sick to my stomach.

My grandmother was not a "happy camper" with my grandfather. Me, I was just an innocent child. Maybe that is why my grandfather, after a very intense conversation, had to put up his tobacco in the barn away from me and my grandmother. I don't think I ever saw my grandfather chew after that.

Anyway, back to the story. Since my grandparents had to supplement their income, they raised chickens for companies that processed them for sale. They would spend the next 6 to 12 weeks babysitting approximately 500 or so little chickens. This babysitting involved feeding, watering, and keeping them warm in the wintertime.

One rule was not to disturb the chickens by chasing them. Ok, I must admit I didn't listen. Those poor chickens were at my mercy and enjoyment.

In general, when a chicken got hurt or the

other chickens turned on this poor chicken, my grandfather would relegate this chicken to the yard to fend for its own survival.

However, one got its revenge. One of these "feather" animals decided to live. It reminded me of the one who caused it to be deposited outside in the yard. This chicken survived because it had a mangled leg and walked around like a pirate. I decided to call it "Peg Leg Pete." Such an innovative name. Well, that whole summer, that "Peg Leg Monster" chased me all over the yard. It soon became apparent that all it wanted to do was peck my legs, which it did a couple of times. However, the day of reckoning arrived when my grandmother decided to have fried chicken for dinner one night. The comment was made at the dinner table that this was the toughest chicken she ever cooked.

Even though I talk about this as a special time in my life, I didn't relish walking 50 yards in the rain or cold to visit the outdoor "facility." I avoided tobacco of any kind and got flashbacks of "Peg Leg Pete" when I saw a chicken on the rotisserie in the store.

Little League and Tobacco

As good as the foundation I received through the TV series, those years were tough on a "dorky" kid. My grammar school was full of not doing well on my grades and having to wear black horn-rim glasses as thick as "coke bottles," which, to my dismay, I had broken on the playground one day. When I went home, I got the punishment that you get for doing stupid stuff. What is worse, the next day, we were having our school pictures taken. Since my parents didn't have the money and time to fix my glasses, they taped them together with white medical adhesive tape. When I had my school picture made, I was the kid with his glasses taped together. This screamed of "dork" ... of course, my mother was proud of that grammar school picture. "There is my son, there ... the one with his glasses taped together and his hair sticking straight up."

During this time, I was convinced that I needed to play Little League baseball. Now remember, the thick glasses ... I was forbidden to wear my glasses during outside activities, remembering the grammar school picture episode. I was put in the outfield, but that made no difference which position because I didn't fare well. Every time a fly ball came for me to catch, it would hit me on the head, arm, leg, or any other part of my body. Finally, after multiple attempts for me to catch the ball, I was reassigned as the catcher. This worked out fine for me because my job was simple ... stop the ball. If I caught the ball, that was fine with the coach. If I didn't catch the ball but stopped it with my body, that was fine also. I lasted only one season, mainly because I couldn't see the ball to hit it.

How many of you have an older sibling who didn't want their younger brother/sister to be around? I so wanted to be a part of my brother's activities. I became a "patsy" for him and his friend Eddie. Eddie was trouble for me; he loved setting me up for failure. He knew how much I wanted to be accepted. One day, my brother and Eddie asked me if I wanted to go with them and smoke some tobacco. What they called tobacco was rabbit tobacco or merely weed. Ok, here is where the "dork" comes out ... there is no such thing. It was a WEED! I wanted so badly to be a part of my brother's friends, so I said, "sure." I had to smoke the tobacco first If I wanted to be with the older boys. This should have been a "red flag." The cowboys on TV always licked the paper when they rolled their cigarettes before lighting up. So, not to look stupid, which was easy for me to do, I rolled my generous helping of the weed (tobacco) in a piece of notebook paper. Now, licking the paper didn't work on notebook paper, so I did the next best thing … I used Scotch tape to hold the paper together. Boy, was this a disaster. I was able to get a couple of drags on my "weed" before the flames from the paper and tape reached my face. The rest of this event culminated in me getting sick and receiving punishment for both my brother and me. Why did I get punished? I guess it was due to being a "dork."

Growing up is always a statement of "I can't wait until I'm 16 years old." My mother used to tell me not to wish my life away. Of course, she followed up her words of wisdom with, "If ifs and buts were candy and nuts, we'd all have a Merry Christmas." Now that I'm older, I really understand what she was telling me. I had to go through all of the preceding just to enter into another phase of my life with its unique challenges. I refuse to use the term "dork," but it could be replaced with "D _ _ b," "A _ _ ," or "DA."

Teen Years

First Date

When I turned 16, I got my driver's license. Freedom at last. My first date was at McDonald's for french fries and a drink. No movie, just McDonalds, and I had to have my date home by 9 pm. Eventually, I progressed to a full date. Pick her up by 5 pm, go roller-skating, stop by McDonald's, and then go home by 10 pm. Now, this is where I strayed off the straight and narrow. We had been dating for about 6 months when we went to my junior/senior dance. Oh, my date was beautiful. I couldn't keep my eyes off her, which is where the problem started. Back then, the front seats were bench-style seats. This way, my date could slide over next to me so we could be close (stupidity at 16 is a constant). This way, I could put my right arm on her shoulder and drive with my left hand on the steering wheel. This was so cool! Well, to some degree, I was still a dork. The car I was driving was a 1954 Cadillac four-door Fleetwood. It had tail lights like shark fins, and the front bumper resembled two-pointed things that looked like big artillery shells, and the front grill had little square openings which reminded me of a waffle iron; however, I was still driving on a date with my girlfriend. What could go wrong?

I met my girlfriend at the local roller-skating rink. Our dates were initially to go to the skating rink and home. What follows is still fresh in my mind.

I was a one-girl man. I was not cool enough to be able to date multiple girls. As I look back on this, I realize that it was a good thing. Many of my friends got into trouble trying to balance dating two to three girls over a weekend. The big thing for me was to go "steady." Again, this could be a good thing and a bad thing.

While taking my date home, we had to go down a two-lane, curvy, blacktop road. By mistake, my right hand brushed against her right breast. Now, this was like being hit with an electric current. My eyes were not on the road but where my right hand had landed. However, in all the commotion, I never took my eyes off her ... as I crossed the center line, still staring at her ... as I crossed over the wrong side of the road, still staring at her ... as I went into the ditch, still staring at her ... then fate had me look up and realized I was in the middle of a corn field mowing down corn stalks at 45 miles per hour. I hit the brakes, and this 'boat" of a car did two 360-degree turns. When we finally stopped, the dust off the corn stalks was slowly rising in front of my headlights. A light came on in a nearby farmhouse. (I think it was their cornfield.) I quickly drove through the cornfield until I was on a dirt road, which led me back to the blacktop road. We finished our trip to her house in silence, with her sitting on her side of the front seat. It wasn't too long after that when we decided to date others.

Ah, but this is not where the story ends, is it ever? Thinking I was in the clear. I got my date home by curfew time and made it back to my house, thinking, oh yea, no longer a dork ... then the sun rose the next morning, and my confident life was changed when my mother woke me up and told me in no uncertain terms to go outside and see my stepfather. Ok, now picture this ... the front grill with the small openings was filled with dirt, grass, and parts of corn stalks. Not a pretty site. But that is not all. If you have ever seen the Wizard of Oz, then you will notice an eerie likeness to the straw man character. There were corn stalks hanging from underneath the car and wheel wells. True to being a "dork," my first words out of my mouth were, "How did the dirt and corn stalks come to be on and under the car?" My stepfather looked at me and said, "I don't want to know or hear your story that I will not accept. You are grounded for two weeks, with no dates, no driving the car, and no having your friends pick you up to go out."

My all-knowing brother provided me with words that gave me hope that I would not be in "no dating hell" forever." If you are going to park with your date, check out the location before you go, and don't, I repeat, don't drive with one hand."

I say again ... dork!

I can say that my teen years were unique times. I survived my first date in the family car. I got lucky that they didn't bury me in that cornfield. We had the Vietnam War and the draft. I didn't go directly to college because my parents could not afford the tuition. However, I was able to go to the local Technical-Vocational school to study Mechanical Technology.

Due to my episode with the cornfield, my mother decided to manage my dating in a very unique way. Now that I look back on this, my mother knew how to make sure that I didn't go "all the way" and get a young girl pregnant. Here's the deal she told me (not necessarily a deal). If I was going to "park" with my girlfriend, then my mother wanted me to park in (on?) the driveway. Mother told me that the only thing I had to do was to come into the house and let her know I was outside. Just think this way: Mother got what she wanted, and I didn't. That really put a damper on any extracurricular activity that my girlfriend and I may have wanted ... sigh!

My First Beer

I grew up in a household that had plenty of alcohol. My parents would have friends over to watch football, cook out on the grill, and drink. Their beer of choice was Schlitz beer. I was in the 12th grade back then, and Coke Cola was my drink of choice. Even to this day, I still remember the alcohol-fueled arguments and slamming of doors. This time in my life shaped my future drinking habits of moderation. The one rule my parents had when their friends came over to party was no driving home. They were expected to spend the night.

Eventually, I was able to get my driver's license, and I was ready to go places without asking my parents to take me there. Eventually, I could only go to the roller skate rink and back home. The skating rink was where I became friends with Duane Brown (Wiener) and Buddy Jones. They were considered the bad boys of the area, and for some unknown reason, they took a shine on me. Lucky that they did.

Eventually, I turned 17, and I was 'testing my wings" on being a 'bad boy." My friends were already there. On Friday nights, we would go down to the local liquor and beer store and buy six packs of beer. The store would sell us beer with no questions asked. Now, I know it is not right to buy alcohol under the age of 21. Now, back in the '60s, we didn't think about drinking and driving. That all said, the beer of choice for us was the small Miller Highlife pony bottles. We would each get a six-pack of the Miller pony bottles. We then went to McDonalds and bought a sack full of hamburgers. You see, the only way I could drink beer was to wash it down with the hamburger. That should have been a "red flag" for me not to drink beer.

This lesson was further made clear the night Duane bought us three six-packs of Schlitz beer. Of course, we had to have hamburgers. Well, since the Schlitz beer did not come in small bottles, I could not drink my six-pack. Well, being an enterprising young man, I wasn't going to throw two cans away. So, when I got home, I went to the woods behind the house and covered them up with leaves and tree branches. Now then, the next time my parents went out of town, I could still have my beer. Now that I look back at that night, it is evident that I didn't think this through. You see, all of this transpired during the winter. I was excited to have a cold beer. It all fell apart when I used a beer can opener, no hamburgers needed, and I took a big swallow of beer. Little did I know that when you freeze and thaw out a can of beer multiple times, it is undrinkable. That first swallow had the texture of raw oysters … thick and slimy. Yep, another lesson learned! I will drink a beer every now and then, but not without thinking back to those two episodes.

Mid-Life Years

Navy Days

I graduated from high school in 1965. Yes, I'm that old. I then entered the local technical school to take a two-year course in mechanical technology. During this two-year span of time, my older brother got drafted into the US Army. A close friend and I decided before we graduated from technical school to join the US Navy. This negated the two of us being drafted, so in September of 1967, we "shipped out," as the saying goes.

This was a tremendous change that I was not expecting. My mother was a "cupcake" when compared to the navy. No more sleeping in; nobody asks you what you want for dinner, and you can't say, "I made a mistake and want to go home." Yes, joining the military was a tremendous change for me.

I had enlisted for a 6-year hitch by cheating on my eye exam. When the doctor was not looking, I memorized the eye chart. I don't think one could do that now. We had one chart with all the letters, nothing like what we have now. I was proud that I pulled a "fast one." However, later I would come to regret this. When I finally got to the Navy Nuclear Power School in Bainbridge, Maryland, I discovered that there would be a LOT of math, including calculus. I have never been good at math stuff. I was able to slip by on my two-year technical school courses. But now it was time to "belly up to the bar." If I didn't pass ANY of the tests during the one-year of my navy school year, I would be reassigned to another ship that was not nuclear-powered. The catch was I would still have my 6-year obligation. Bummer! With the help of some of my shipmates, I found out that the only way to get out of the 6-year obligation was to fail my final physical. So this time, I read the eye chart as I should have. My 6-year obligation was reduced to four years.s   Yea! Within 6 weeks, I was on my way to my next assignment, USS Boxer LPH-4, homeported in Norfolk, Virginia, for four months. This was great because I could go home on the weekends when I did not have watch responsibilities. It was during this time that I got married to my high school sweetheart. This union started out well, but with me soon to be gone to sea for at least 6 months, it was a trying time for both of us.

Of course, I learned some bad habits while in the navy. I became an expert at choosing descriptive four-letter words as nouns, adjectives, adverbs, etc., which my mother would not have approved. Eventually, I got transferred to my next assignment,

I was assigned to a Destroyer Escort, DE-1028. USS VanVoorhis. It was a small ship of approximately 300+ feet long and 35 feet wide at the beam. When the sea was rough, we bounced around like a plastic fishing cork. But the most annoying thing I discovered was the fact that I have motion sickness. What a rude discovery, especially since I will be on this ship for another 3+ years. I reported aboard on a Friday, and then the ship got underway for four months. That evening, the navy cook served sloppy joe sandwiches with milk to drink. After about two hours, I was heaving over the side of the ship, and just think, I had 3+ years of this. Thank goodness they had a navy corpsman on board, and he gave me a supply of Dramamine until I could buy some at the PX when I got back into port.

Life aboard a ship, and a small ship at that, is ... boring while out at sea. It was during this time that I learned about smoking and drinking coffee and other beverages. The one thing that I truly missed was sleep. When not doing work, I would be in my bunk, sleeping.

Because I joined during the Vietnam era, things such as security and the public displeasure with the military got so bad that it was suggested that I not wear my uniform when I left the ship to go on liberty or home on leave. I was and am proud of my service to my country and to the navy. Since my brother was in the army's 1st Cavalry in Vietnam, I also felt a strong obligation to him to do my part. This feeling is stronger today than it was in yesteryear. Since I was on a Destroyer Escort, our main responsibilities were to escort ships across the Atlantic Ocean or wherever they might be going. We were there to guard against a foreign adversary that might be on the surface or below.

Sea Story

The one thing that the navy insisted on was that we always go on liberty in groups of two, especially overseas. On one deployment to the Mediterranean, we ported to Naples, Italy. My first foreign port! My best friend Ronnie Alexander and I perfected the activities of drinking and smoking. Since both of us were married, female persuasion was not on the menu, even though there were some entrees that looked mighty good! Well, we decided to go "bar hopping." We were going to hit every bar with a US city name. Bad move on our part. First, we didn't realize that there were bars named New York bar, San Francisco bar, Chicago bar, Texas bar, or Boston bar, and I lost count. Our drink that night was a screwdriver. Now, for the uninitiated, a screwdriver drink is vodka and orange juice. But there was a problem: the bartenders had no OJ. Instead, we got an eight oz glass of vodka with three cubes of ice and a slice of orange. I was a lightweight back then, but Ronnie was a seasoned sailor. He ran from bar to bar to have the same drink at each.

The night ended by 8 pm for us. We took the liberty launch (an open-air boat) out to our ship. There were three ships moored there, just like ours. I got my friend to his bunk, and then I crawled into mine. However, I awoke and discovered my friend was nowhere to be found. At the 0730 muster, when Ronnie's name was called out, he didn't respond. The master chief turned to me and asked where's Ronnie. Needless to say, I didn't know, and I promptly tried to explain the whole story from last night. Just then, the quartermaster from one of the sister ships wanted to know if we were missing a sailor. Geez, they found him in somebody else's bunk, which was in the same location as his was on our ship. Ronnie had slipped back over to the city, and after a couple of hours, the shore patrol brought him back. He then proceeded to find his bunk and crawled into it … on the wrong ship. I got my liberty for the next week cancelled because I didn't make sure he was in his bunk asleep. You just can't trust a drunk sailor overseas drinking screwdrivers. To this day, I can't touch one without thinking of Ronnie.

During my everyday life, I meet many military veterans. Since my brother, father, stepfather, and close friends served, I feel a kinship with them. The other day, when I arrived at my favorite watering hole, I sat down next to this individual. He was dressed in stained khaki trousers, a long-sleeved light blue shirt, a black leather vest, dirty work boots, and a leather Australian outback hat. He was unshaven and wore black glasses. He did give off a unique image. I was raised not to judge a book by its cover, so I held my reservations and sat down next to him. He immediately introduced himself. His name was Bill, and he started a conversation with me by asking if I served. My response was a very proud yes. I told him I served in the navy during the Vietnam era. He responded that he was in the Navy Seabees and served with "boots on the ground" in Vietnam. We discussed our individual experiences in the navy. I recounted to him a time when, while traveling home from Atlanta, Georgia, to Birmingham, Alabama, I was able to witness one of the most touching examples of honor to one country and fellow servicemen. I had noticed a highly decorated enlisted soldier waiting to board the same flight as me. Since I was in the business class seat, I approached him and offered to swap seats. (He was in coach class.) He was polite and stoic when he responded to my offer. He was on duty escorting a fellow comrade home. It took me a minute to understand what he was saying. As the saying goes, no soldier is left behind, and no soldier comes home alone. He was escorting a fallen comrade back home. After we deplaned, I was able to find a window in the concourse where I could watch the ritual. As I stood there in silence, other travelers joined me. Eventually, a hearse pulled up right after a military vehicle arrived with eight servicemen. Each one knew their duty and performed it well. The flagged draped coffin emerged from the belly of the plane, with each serviceman taking on the honor of moving their fallen comrade to the hearse. As tears welled up in my eyes, I couldn't help but think of my brother, who suffered in Vietnam. Even though it's been some time since that night, every Memorial Day, I wonder about the impact this fallen soldier's life had on his family and on our nation.

My experiences do not come close to those of my friend, Andy. He was in the Navy Seabees during Vietnam. He told me that there was nothing like doing construction work with the possibility of being shot. During our conversation, I discovered that he had spent 20 years in the navy and then retired. I tipped my hat to him.

Now it's time to "pass the baton" to the future generations. The son of one of our friends joined the air force, and his dad invited another mutual friend (who retired from the army) and me to celebrate his leaving for boot camp. Of course, we "old guard" gave him all kinds of pointers on how to survive boot camp ... no laughing or smiling at anything the instructor said or did. We then lifted our glasses up and toasted to him and his future. We then stood erect and straight and saluted him. This young man joining the military gives me faith that we are in good hands.

Later Years

Relationships

I'm currently on my second round of being married. It took my first marriage to figure out what I did wrong and how to correct it the next time around. As I have mentioned before, everybody has a story that contains some happy moments and some sad ones. I know you have heard the saying that you need a little salt and pepper to make life interesting. I'm not different than anybody else.

My daughter and I went through some tough times with her mother/my wife. Well, let's just say our financial situation was not the best. Like most newlyweds, we lived day by day. As the saying goes, "robbing Peter to pay Paul." We tried everything to right the boat. Nothing seemed to work. Our personalities clashed on how to stop the "bleeding of money" from our accounts. I became more adamant by tightening control of the finances, whereas she became more allusive and withdrawn. Many things transpired over the last 12 years of our marriage. We endured the writing of checks to cover checks even though the money was not there. Meeting lawyers to work through the possibility of her going to jail for embezzling money from her work. The sad part of this was that my daughter loved her mother, and when her mother involved her in our problems, this started the souring of their relationship. She was involved in hiding bills, collection notices, etc. I felt that it was my responsibility as the man of the house to do everything in my power to put things right.

We started attending the company-paid marriage counseling. It was during these traumatic times that I discovered that my wife was abused as a child. I never found out what that entailed, but as it was explained to me by the counselor, this history exacerbated the deterioration of our marriage. I'm closer to my daughter more now than in any other part of our lives. When I look back at our time together, I'm proud that we survived and became better individuals. To say the least, I feel that my daughter suffered the most.

As they say, "life moves on." We got divorced, and over the next few years, I was able to pay off all the creditors. The scars are still there. This will be a part of my life that I will draw upon.

Eventually, I met a fine lady who has been sharing my life for the last 30 years. She had also become the surrogate mother for my daughter. All of this led up to a recent conversation my daughter had with one of my wife's sisters. As my daughter explained to me, my sister-in- law was concerned that I might be in financial distress because it appeared that our finances were tight. They wanted to help us out. My daughter's response was that our actions were due to our previous experiences with my first wife. She explained in detail the trials and tribulations I went through with her mother. Basically, now I'm "cash flow" sensitive. My daughter is quick to come to my defense if need be, and I love her loyalty to me.

Now, it must be obvious that not once have I mentioned my current wife. She has covered my back, understands my history, and supports me 100%. My trust in her is unquestionable. This led to the fact that before leaving for my job in Alaska, I agreed to give her complete power of attorney over my finances and health decisions. To this day, my "will" recognizes this responsibility.

I met my future wife at a bowling tournament she was managing. At the time, I had no intentions of getting involved in a serious relationship. Being a single man after 21 years of marriage, going from the house I grew up in, and marrying while still in the navy, I had never experienced living on my own, and I wanted to know what that was like. I was like a dog that had been fenced up most of his life, but finally, I got out of the fence in the yard and was free. I was like that dog running from yard to yard with my nose about an inch off the ground, taking in all new senses. Eventually, I settled down, learning what it was like to live by myself. When we met, I was working on a bowling tournament computer program. I heard that there was a lady who wanted to meet me. While I was working on my computer program, she walked by my door, and our eyes met; that is all she wrote.

We were in our early 40s when we met. We dated for three years, her living in Birmingham, Alabama, and I in Augusta, Georgia. We saw each other every weekend. I would drive over to Birmingham, and the next weekend, she would come to Augusta.

My current wife is from New Jersey, Bruce

Springsteen territory, Seaside Heights boardwalk, and Coney Island style hotdogs. She is independent, totally capable of taking care of herself, and willing to speak her mind. The following makes my point. We had been dating for a while, and we had a "conversation" about where this relationship was going. I'm not sure what prompted this conversation, but it must have been someone or something that put a bug in her ear. The conversation goes something like this. "I know about you boys from the South. Smooth talking, polite, opening doors, and the need to take care of their woman; you know, marry her and become the 'man' of the house." She continued, "I have a good job, I have a good income, I have financed my house on my own, I have money in my retirement fund, and I have my cat. As far as I'm concerned, we can keep this relationship as is, seeing each other every other weekend, and you don't need to marry me to make me an honest woman." Now, being the "red-blooded" young stud (debatable), I thought I hit the jackpot! Nope, she put me in my place. I finally realized later that when you tell someone they can't do something, they will go out of their way to change it. All of this transpired during the spring ... I proposed to her in June of that same year. She really is "smart." I have met my match .... However, I'm not sure she would fit the description of a Southern Belle.

There are many differences between ladies from the North and South. To understand these differences, the following example happened to me before I married my Jersey girl.

We in the South cook with Crisco, lard, or bacon grease because it gives the food flavor, and to be honest, that's the way it has always been. It is slowly changing, but frying is the way to go. Now, up North, frying food is a nonstarter. It is either baked or grilled, and veggies "Aldente." They say we overcook, whereas we would say they like it crunchy. In the South, we say we are going to grill some hamburgers, whereas up North, if they want hamburgers, they call it barbecue. If you are from the South, you know what a barbeque is.

While we were dating, my future wife (second) wanted to impress me by cooking some fried chicken with mashed potatoes, biscuits, and gravy. When I got home from work, my daughter was already there for dinner. The table was set, fried chicken on a platter, mashed potatoes in a bowl, and a side of gravy and canned biscuits. I took my first bite of mashed potatoes, which tasted different. I wanted to be tactful and told her they were good when, in fact, they tasted something like vanilla flavoring. My daughter was not as gracious as I was. My soon-to-be wife stated that the recipe called for buttermilk. Since we didn't have any, she used some French Vanilla coffee creamer. The surprises didn't end there. I picked up a piece of fried chicken, and low and behold, it was burnt to a black cider on the bottom. As it was explained through her tears, she had never cooked with a black iron skillet, and things had gotten a little out of control. I must say that the opposite side of the chicken was a nice golden brown ... the burnt side down.

I finally broke down and asked her if she would marry me. After all, I had to take her off the "available list" as there were others waiting in line behind me to take her out.

Our engagement started out while I was unemployed. Now, I might not be the smartest guy on the street, but I do know that weddings cost a lot of money, that is, if you don't go to the justice of the peace. Because I had a lot of baggage from my first wedding, I wanted to show my newly engaged fiancé that I was innovative and conscious of money. To do this, I came up with a good way to save us money. I suggested that we buy a roll of movie coupon tickets and send them out to the invited wedding guest list. We could have assorted drinks and food. We could have bar food so we could give three food tickets and one drink ticket. Now, I thought this was a fantastic way to save money. Do you want to guess how my suggestion was received? I got the "hairy eyeball" and a firm, "what were you thinking?" To cut the story short, we got married, my wife paid for the wedding (since I was unemployed), and everybody went home happy!

Now, you should be asking what is a "hairy eyeball." Let me put it this way: when your significant other does something stupid, there is a look that speaks a thousand words. I have also heard this look called "the mom look." I prefer the "hairy eyeball."

Now, whenever someone asks me how long we've been married, I make sure to give an answer that will satisfy the "faint of heart" when this question is asked. Are you ready? Make sure you have paper and a pen in hand to write it down. You will want to be able to answer the same way without hesitation. A pause that is too long will give the impression that you are grasping at anything to say that will keep you out of the doghouse. Here we go... I put on my sincere, happy face and, without any hesitation, while looking at my wife, say, "Not long enough," and then smile. Now you can imagine the look and the whispers my wife gives me, *"You really don't know how long, do you? I'll let this slide for now. Just wait until later."*

Regardless, I must say that I have hit the "jackpot." She is a wonderful lady, especially when she must put up with some of my antics, coupons aside

At our wedding, I was stressed, which resulted in me not getting my lines straight during the ceremony. I specifically requested that the minister give me short, simple lines to quote for the ceremony. Well, this didn't go well. When the words came up to "pledge my love," what I said didn't come to our. I repeated, "I pledge to my wife my UN-faithful love. "You could hear the gasps from the attendees and the looks I got from the minister asking me if I wanted to go back over what I said, "No, keep moving; we are just about done." I got the "hairy eyeball" from my soon-to-be wife. My best man told me that I got a winner for a wife because most women would have stopped the ceremony and made a big deal. What? I just slipped up a little.

There are many stories about my life that I recount (probably too many times). I like to look at them as the spices that give meaning to one's life.

There is one story that I recount routinely. In fact, my wife declared that if she had a nickel every time I told the story, she would be rich. Now, I think she is exaggerating a little ... maybe one hundred dollars, come on, now rich?

Well, here is the story that she talks about. My friend Steve and I were managing a bowling tournament across three states. Now we were good, and a lot of people made money. In fact, we made money before paying our room rate, food, and bar bill. Yea, we tended to celebrate before the roll-off on Sunday.

One weekend, we had a tournament in Milledgeville, Georgia. We had to leave early on Saturday to drive back to Augusta, Georgie, for another bowling tournament. Now, by the time we left, we had already exceeded the capacity of our bladders. We normally traveled the back roads to Augusta, Georgia. We were running behind time, so when we came upon a lone crossroad with no lights and four-way stop signs, and since I was driving, I made a management decision. I told Steve we were not going to pull off the road and relieve ourselves, but instead, we would leave the car in first gear. We opened our doors and ran alongside the slowly moving car and relieved ourselves. When done, we jumped back into the car and sped off. Such a wonderful night!

Yes, those were the days.

Believe it or not, she still married me with all my baggage. Now, whenever there is a discussion about when we were married and what it is like to start over at that late stage in life, I can explain in one word:" Fantastic." Both of us had to go through a lot of "trials and tribulations," but the journey was worth it.

Job Jar

There was a time after I met my current wife when we worked on her house. It was enjoyable to have that ability to come in and fix something that she couldn't or wouldn't do. She had this uncanny ability to get male friends to complete projects around the house for her. Just a smile and a flirty attitude can make a man do anything for the lady.

She created a way of capturing the projects she wanted to accomplish ... she called it a "Job jar." This jar was one that at one time contained pickles, pickled eggs, or pickled sausages. The once-held jar that these gourmet eats usually sat on the corner of the bar at a local "watering hole." They usually were sold for $1 each. They were nasty. These pickles, eggs, and sausages were so nasty that they wreaked havoc on one's bodily functions (usually the next day).

Anyway, back to the story. She was able to convince one of her previous boyfriends to find one of these jars for her. Whenever she was going through her house, or she saw something that she wanted done or something fixed, she would write it on a piece of paper and put it in a jar. She taped directions on the side of the jar. Whenever you get bored, just go to the job jar, reach in, select a piece of paper, pull it out, and read what needs to be done. This was like opening a fortune cookie and reading what was on the piece of paper. You never know what you are going to get. When we started dating, I realized that a lot of these projects were the ones I would be doing. I'm not a big fan of a work plan on a piece of paper from a pickle jar full of pieces of paper. On top of that, these pieces of paper smelled a lot like pickled eggs... nasty. I tried not to pick a project that would be too complex.

I finally just ignored 'the job jar." As time passed and we got married, the "Job Jar" got relegated to a closet. When my parents came to visit us for a week or so, my father complained that he wanted something to do. He was not a fan of watching afternoon TV soaps and quickly got bored; thus, the Job Jar was resurrected from the closet.

When they came over to visit us, we explained that we had projects that needed to be addressed. Examples of the projects would be cutting grass, cleaning out the front flower bed, and washing the car. Beverley gave him the same direction she gave me. Whatever you pulled from that jar was the project to be completed.

Well, my father would go to the Job jar and pull out a piece of paper with the project, look at it, and then tell my mother, "No, I'm not doing that," and instead of putting it back inside the jar, he threw it away. After a couple of visits over to our house to spend some time with us, Beverley noticed that the pieces of paper in the Job jar were getting smaller. She got concerned and started questioning both me and my parents about what happened to them.

Well, my parents explained to her that if she knew the project couldn't be accomplished, then there was no need to put the piece of paper back into the jar. The reasoning was that if the project was not doable or you did not want to do it, it would still be that way the next time it was pulled from the jar.

My mother was not exempt from this thinking. She had a habit of going through the refrigerator and looking at the expiration dates. There is a current commercial out now featuring Aunt Jenny checking the dates on the product and saying, "Expired, expired, expired." That's what my parents would do, and they cleaned out our refrigerator cause my wife had some stuff growing fuzz and mold on them in there. The upside is that when we got ready to move, the Job jar and fridge were cleaned out, and we basically left them behind for the new homeowners.

Christmas Trees

My wife loves Christmas. Picture this: the year – any year – Octobers in Birmingham, AL; I look around, and all I see are Christmas decorations. This is more than trees. It is the ornaments, bells hanging on doorknobs, cabinet pull handles, and lampshades. I wonder when it will happen ... that is when all of this will disappear. No need to fool myself. I know exactly when I will be able to bring them down ... after Groundhog Day. Yes, that is correct ... Groundhog Day! There are little figurines everywhere. These things are even in the bathroom! I can't even go in there because they are standing there staring at me. Creepy ....

I think this affection towards Christmas trees and decorations started with my wife's first husband. As the story goes, my wife refused to take the living room Christmas tree down until her first husband took the time to sit in front of the tree with a glass of wine and listen to the record player she got from him on Christmas day. She told a friend about her situation, and in turn, her friend contacted the local newspaper about her plight. They requested and were granted an interview, and she recounted her story. It wasn't too long after the interview appeared in the Lifestyles section of the local newspaper that she got her glass of wine and music in front of the Christmas tree. From that one incident, she started decorating and decorating and decorating. Fast forward to when we met.

Our first Christmas as a couple should have been a foretelling of things to come. We started putting up the tree lights, and I followed the tradition of how my family decorated; we draped the lights. Wrong! Her family wrapped most of the tree branches. Ok, I can deal with the lights, but now, here comes the ornaments. As with my family's tradition, I'm used to a 6-foot tree, two strands of lights, and three boxes of 12 ornaments. Done! Yippee ... wrong! There were so many ornaments on the tree that I thought I heard the tree moan from all the stuff hanging on it. Ok, I can deal with the ornaments. Alas, we (I, in this case) can sit back and enjoy the fruits of our labor... Wrong! Her house had seven Christmas trees … artificial. I threw my hands up and shouted, "Uncle"! I learned one thing for sure: open a bottle of wine, sit down, and let her do her thing. I didn't want her going behind me to correct my mistakes so she could do it her way. Don't get me wrong, I love her dearly, and she has the "decorating eye," and when she is through, everything looks great.

We then moved to a house that we called our own. A two-story monster, and much to my dismay, this house had four bedrooms, three bathrooms, an entertainment room, a dining room, a breakfast room, a great room, and a screened porch. Guess what was in store for me at Christmas time. Each room, apart from the bathrooms and great room, had 6-foot Christmas trees. The bathrooms had small trees on the vanities, and the great room had a 12-foot monster tree. The screened porch had a four-foot tree, which she changed out based on the current holiday, Easter, Valentine, 4th of July, and Thanksgiving.

Keeping in line with the wine and decorating

mindset, I started having box wine. While she decorated the trees, I realized that I needed to help, so the deal we made was I would get the trees from the storage shed and put them up. I envy those individuals who put up one tree and take it down the weekend after the New Year celebration. This philosophy worked out just fine. I got into a routine, and I knew what to expect. Then … we moved to our 3rd "forever house." It is smaller, but the trees go up, and the decorations come out … along with the box of wine. This has happened every year since we got married. I have no expectation that this will change; in fact, I hope it doesn't.

Alaska

When we got married, I was between jobs. Between the job jar and looking for work, I stayed busy. Since I was in quality assurance and inspection, there were no jobs that fit this description in Birmingham, AL. Every day, my job was to use the internet to look for a job that met my credentials. Eventually, I was offered a job in Anchorage, Alaska. I couldn't wait to tell my wife that I landed a plum job. It was to establish a quality program for the oil pipeline. This was during the Exxon Valdez mishap. Well, when she got home, we got ourselves a drink and an Atlas. It was soon evident that there was no coming home on the weekends. It is 4,274 miles or 2 days 20 hrs. Realization set in; we hadn't been married for even five months, and now I'm in Alaska for at least a year. Well, we settled on me taking the job.

I went to work with my best man at my wedding. He is an outstanding and devoted friend. We worked on many contracts together and traveled to many places to keep the money coming in for the family. While we were on a contract in Anchorage, Alaska, we shared a 2-bedroom, 2-bath apartment. At the day's end, we would sit around the small table and have our daily "toddy" before dinner. We called it the "table of enlightenment". During one of these profound sessions, we came up with the following. As you will see, a little of the "happy juice" was involved with its creation.

Deja vu: Strange feeling. I have been here before.

Devu ja: I can't believe this stuff is happening.

Vuja de: Strange feeling. I have not been here before.

Jade vu: Strange feeling. I'm going back again.

Vude ja: Strange feeling this stuff has happened before.

Javu de: Strange feeling. I think I'm going back again but I'm not sure I've ever been there before.

Veda ju: The act of strangeness or the condition of being strange.

Another day, at the "table of enlightenment," we were discussing utter detachment and the impact upper management can have on our daily working lives. To this end, we set out on our mystical journey to find something that describes this impact. Below is what we found.

In the beginning was the plan and then came the assumptions.

And the assumptions were without form, and the plan was completely without substance, and the darkness was upon the faces of the workers, and they spoke among themselves, saying, "It is a crock of 'dung,' and it stinketh."

And the workers went unto their supervisors and sayeth, "It is a pail of 'dung,' and none may abide the odor thereof."

And the supervisors went unto their managers and sayeth unto them,

"It is a container of excrement, and it is very strong,

such that none may abide by it." And the managers went unto their directors and sayeth,

"It is a vessel of fertilizer, and none may abide its strength."

And the directors spoke amongst

themselves, saying one to another,
"It contains that which aids plant growth,
and it is very strong.'
And the directors went unto the vice
presidents, sayeth unto them,
"It promotes growth and is very powerful.'
And the vice presidents went unto the
president and sayeth unto him,
"This new plan will actively promote the
growth and efficiency of this company and
the areas in particular."
And the president looked upon the plan and
saw that it was good,
and the plan became policy.
This is how *(please insert your word preference
here)* ... happens!

This is what happens when you work in Alaska during the winter when there are limited hours of daylight.

I was able to see Alaska in all its seasons, which are really just the ... winter and summer, with spring and fall. It would be very easy to miss them if you sleep too long.

Everything you might have heard about Alaska is true. The TV series called Northern

Exposure is right on point. I got to see the northern lights, ice fog, black bears, and a moose on the road next to my apartment.

There is a strong pioneering feeling among those who live in Alaska, and they do not want anybody from the lower 48 telling them what to do. Since my friend and I were on the same job, we were able to come home every 5th week for 10 days. I would leave on Friday afternoon and arrive in Birmingham at 7:30 am on Saturday. Going back, I would leave at noon on the following Sunday and arrive nine hours later the day.

I was able to have my wife fly up rather than me fly to Birmingham. Just like me, she was amazed after she left the airport. This trip was in the fall or early winter. The town had already started decorating for winter. They put up strings of lights everywhere. I was told that they would stay up all winter. The main reason for the lights was to combat depression and suicide, which are common in Alaska. This can be attributed to the lack of sunlight during the winter months.

My favorite watering hole in Anchorage was and is Darwin's Theory. Odd name, isn't it? Well, the owner himself marches to a different drumbeat. This bar reminds me of an old western bar. You can read about Darwin a little later in this book. Since my time in Alaska focused on the Alaska pipeline, there was a wider variety of customers at Darwin's. You will see everyday people, attorneys, people from the bush (those who live in cabins away from civilization), and Alaska Airlines pilots, just to mention a few. Speaking of Alaska Airlines pilots, I will have to tread lightly here. On one of our visits to Anchorage, Alaska, we went to Darwin's Theory. It is a small, bare, horseshoe shape downtown bar. It's easy to carry on a conversation with the patrons on the other side of the bar. There was a pilot with thick, black, curly hair. Guess what type of hair my wife likes? Yep, thick, black, curly hair.

After a couple of drinks, my wife commented that she would love to run her fingers through his hair. My comment to her was, well, go over and ask him if you can run your fingers through his hair. I try to be philosophical about this. I figured if she wanted to leave me for a pilot with thick, black, curly hair, then it would be the best I know now. She asked me again if I was Ok with this, and I said yes and kissed her. She got up from the bar stool, went around to the pilot, and asked him if she could run her fingers through his hair. I think the guy was flabbergasted. His comment was, "What would your husband say?" He looked over at me, and I just smiled. This is as "racy" as it gets. The pilots quickly paid their tabs and left in a hurry. As I have said before, the bar is a potpourri of personalities.

You Meet the Strangest People at a Bar

I've always been a loyal fan of Cheers. A dysfunctional family it may be, but it is still a family nonetheless. I have always tried to find a place that I could visit and feel like I was part of a Cheers-type family. Hey, it's Norm and Cliff …. Did you know that at Boston Airport, there is a Cheers bar with two wooden individuals sitting at the bar? Yep, Cliff and Norm. The owner had them wired, so if you pushed the button in front of Norm, it would say, "Hey Sam, I'll take another beer." Such a novel way to get people into the bar.

When I moved into my current neighborhood, I had to find a local "watering hole" that was close to home. So, just in case, if I've had too many, I could still get a ride home. Just like the Cheers bar, when I walked into the bar, my drink of choice was already waiting for me. As with any bar, we have various characters there to entertain us. Yes, I was one of those characters. The following is just a sampling of some of the events that usually occur. Remember, the names have been changed to protect—not the innocent but those in attendance without the knowledge of their significant other.

Recently, while I was having my beverage, I looked at the other patrons and wondered what their lives were like. Everybody has a story, some good and some bad, some interesting and some boring. It's almost a requirement that you at least recognize the patron(s) next to you.

You will quickly realize whether they want to carry on a conversation or not. If they don't, then back to my beverage.

While sitting at the bar, a gentleman and his wife sauntered up to the bar and sat down to my right. They ordered their drinks and introduced themselves to me. They were probably in their 70s, very pleasant, easy-going. Their story is that he and his wife had been in Florida and were traveling back to their home in Arizona. I noticed the man's ball cap that he was in the army and a Vietnam veteran, so we struck up a conversation. I found out that we had a lot in common due to being in the military at the same time. He told me that he was given the nickname "Doc Rod" while in Vietnam. He explained how he got that name, but for the life of me, I don't remember it now. As we conversed, the bar was getting very noisy, and I found it hard to understand parts of our conversation. Now, this is where we need to take a sidebar. I have had a hearing deficiency from my days in the navy, so I carry hearing aids, which I don't routinely wear (not cool). My wife tells me I have "selective hearing." "What? I didn't hear you." She shakes her head, and I just smile. As I explained to my military friend, the reason I don't wear them is because they work too well. With my hearing aids, I can hear you, but sometimes, I can even hear a fly scratching its nose across the room. That's how powerful these things are, especially if they're not adjusted. Finally, my conversation with my military buddy ends. He and his wife paid their respects and tab and left. And now the seat next to me is open.

"The doctor is in. Next."

The next person to take the seat next to me is a middle-aged man. His name was "Bubba." Really, his parents named him Bubba. I don't understand why they would do such a thing. It reminds me of the country song "A Boy Named Sue." For sure, I don't think anyone would forget the name "Bubba." After the introduction, we started talking about getting older and forgetting people's names. I told Bubba I had a solution to that problem. If I can't remember your name, I'll smile and shake your hand and say, "Hey, dude," or "Hey, chief. How's it going?" That is usually my way of saying I don't remember your name, but I'm going to at least recognize you. For women, this is a different story, and normally, when I'm served by a lady, I will say thanks "darling," and not "sweetheart" or "babe" because those are bad words to say to another woman, especially if your wife is sitting there. Anyway, Bubba was an insurance agent. I didn't ask him which insurance company he worked for because I was afraid it was mine. After a few more drinks, Bubba paid for his tab and was on his way home.

"The doctor is in. Next."

John, the "Turtle Man," comes in and sits down next to me. Nice guy and a regular at the bar. Usually, an individual would have a dog or cat as a pet, but not a turtle. Just in case you are asleep, this gentleman has two large turtles named Ralph and Alice. Now, an obvious question an individual would ask is, "Tell me, John, how did you come up with the names for the turtles?" His response was, "Don't know, just did." These turtles are not small turtles but very large, like a small dog. Then I made the mistake of asking the question, how do you determine the sex of a turtle? (After all, we don't want the turtles to have a mental complex being named the wrong gender.) This opened a whole biological discussion that I was not ready to have. Can't knock him, though; he talks about his "turtles" the same way others may talk about their "comfort cow." Harmless but weird, time to see another patron.

"The doctor is still in. Next." This new patron is an interesting character, and he served in the Navy Seabees. His enlistment time was 10 years until his time was cut short due to an accident in the service. Still wanting to serve his country, he became a Boston police officer. He eventually retired from law enforcement, and now he and his wife are traveling through the US, enjoying the fruits of their labor. During our conversation about our time in the military, he reached into his pocket, and lo and behold, he brought out a challenge coin.

For those of you who have never seen or understood a challenge coin, it has a unique history.

It is a specially designed coin that is given to confirm membership in an organization or group. A challenge coin can also honor a person for a special achievement. They build a close-knit, lasting bond between people who receive them and represent unity. They have a long-standing tradition in military history. As the story goes, if a military or first responder places his challenge coin on the bar and you don't have one to place next to his, then you owe him a drink.

As I thought back to my previous t conversations with my military buddies, I noticed two ladies having a lively talk at the other end of the bar. I wondered what they were discussing, and then I saw the reason for their conversation ... a laptop computer. They were using Facetime/Zoom and were having a conversation with someone else. Being the inquisitive individual I am, I got my beverage and moved down to the end of the bar to investigate. I introduced myself, and within a short period of time and another beverage, I had joined their conversation. It was explained to me that they were two UAB (University Alabama at Birmingham) students working with a team of other students on a thesis about, what else, the people you meet at a bar! They quickly went back to their conversation, and I realized that I was probably going to be a footnote in their thesis. I quickly exited back to my stool as they were immersed in their discussion.

"The doctor is out. Make an appointment for next week."

Finally, this topic must include a discussion of Mary Sue. (Not her real name, but it will do so for now.) She attended the Woodstock Music Festival, and when it was over, she made her way to Anchorage, Alaska, and ended up as the bartender at Darwin's Theory, a hole-in-the-wall of a small bar. She would tell us stories of her days at the festival, which kept us sitting there transfixed and, of course, buying drinks.

Darwin's Theory reminds me of the Toby Keith song "I Love This Bar."

We got winners, We got losers,
Chain-smokers and boozers, We got yuppies,
We got thirsty hitchhikers,
And the girls next door dress up like movie stars.
Hmmm, hmmm, hmmm, hmmm, hmmm
I love this bar ....

Yes, it was that kind of bar. On any given day, you would see corporate attorneys, Alaskan airline pilots, and mountain men with their rifles and pistols. Music was available on an outdated jukebox. If you wanted something to munch on, they had a small popcorn machine with all the free popcorn you wanted, except if you took the last of the popcorn, you had to make the next batch. On Fridays and Saturdays, Mary Sue would make a large pan of lasagna, which she sold for $1 a slice. No big deal, except she always placed a small toy the size of an eraser on the end of a pencil in the lasagna. Whoever got the toy in their slice had to go behind the bar and wash their glasses. I don't remember asking about the condition of the small toy after cooking the lasagna. She could have added it after cooking. However, I can say that the regulars had no problem with the condition of the toy. (Typical of regular 'bar hugging" guests.) I must say that I had the privilege to wash the glasses.

The last notable thing about this special place was the bar's slogan:

"A smart monkey never messes around with another monkey's monkey."

The odd thing about this slogan is that the owner, Darwin himself, was the biggest "tom cat," or should I say "monkey" in town.

Live and learn.

Beam Me Up, Scottie

While I was in Alaska, my wife and I kept Ma Bell in business. We called each other every day. After all, we were newlyweds. Our long-distance bill ran into the hundreds of dollars.

Technology is on a relentless march to make our lives better and easier from generation to generation. I've always heard the comment, "We are doing this to make your life easier." How could anyone have expected the major advances that would change the way we communicate with someone across town or around the world? I think back to my grandparents and the progress they saw in their lives.

My grandparents witnessed the Industrial Revolution, which, to mention a few, brought us the moving assembly line, WWI, and the stock market crash. Little did they know of the pending change coming with communication. No more letters or postcards ....

With all this wonderful technology, communication between humans has forever been changed. Just think, we don't have to call someone to talk; we can just text them, or "FaceTime" or meet someone face-to-face with "Zoom." We now have smart watches to accomplish these tasks. If that wasn't enough, we can take pictures of others and "help us all," even take selfies - for the ones totally absorbed with their looks. Little did we know that the Dick Tracy comic strip developed in 1931 and ran on TV in the 1950s would foretell things to come. This cartoon popularized the two- way radio and was a peek into the future. His watch allowed him to stay in contact with police headquarters. In fact, the Apple Watch looks a lot like the two-way phone that was used in the cartoon. Such a novel idea ....

Early on, the advent of the wall phone was the first step toward the phone as we know it today. The wall phone was usually located at a central location, such as a grocery store within the community, so everyone could use it. The first problem they faced was on which wall they would hang the darn thing.

Eventually, progress continued in the communications world, and we got phones in our houses. However, it was called a "party line."

There was a good chance when you picked up the phone to use it, someone down the street was already using the "party line." That's right, more than one household was assigned to a single telephone line. Now, this was a good thing in that you could use your phone from your house … that is, if "Gabby Gertie" would quit talking and hang up the line.

We have made great strides since then. This occurred over a time span of 40 years, from 1983 with the first commercially available cell phone to now 2023 with a cell phone in every back pocket.

Now, what I want to know is how does that phone stay in the back pocket? Further, how does the phone use your "butt" to dial? Interesting ….

Phone manufacturing companies realize they could make a lot of money by continually selling a new phone (upgrade) to the public. They have us right where they want us. "A new version of our phone is available now for only X dollars." You will notice that I didn't document a dollar amount because it is constantly changing. Remember, this is a phone.

Now, here we are with the "smartphone," which is defined as a portable computer device that combines a telephone and computing function into one unit. We have become addicted to this new device; we just can't put it down. To make my point, when I go with a group to lunch, we sit down and order, and immediately, they go to their smartphones, Facebook, in particular. They are not into "X" or other social media platforms. After we finish our lunch, I look forward to discussing the news of the day, etc.; however, they get hooked to their phones. Oh, to make sure they include everyone in their enjoyment, they take their phone and stick it right in front of your face and say, "Isn't that Kool?!" Lunch is a very enlightening experience for me ... not necessarily for them. There is no help for them. They have already gone over to the dark side.

Let's not forget that we can text on this device. This opens a whole new path for communication. As the story goes, "Why didn't you call me? Texts would have been better." (By the way, you can ignore a text and respond when you are good and ready, which I have been known to do.) I've been told that it's easier to end a conversation with someone when the conversation is not going the way in the right direction.

I've noticed that the younger generation would rather text than call someone on the phone. Texting is the main communication method. Some time ago, while working on a large project, I was assigned eight team members, all in their late twenties. One day, I got a text message from one team member asking me if I wanted to go to lunch with the rest of the team. This is not an unusual request. However, I thought it was odd how the request was made. After a minute, I turned around and looked at the team member and said, "Sure, why not?" Why didn't they just ask me the question rather than text me?

We can't be away from our phones, oh, excuse me, communicating devices. We need to make sure that if someone calls or sends a text, we will be able to respond; "Why didn't you answer my call?" or "Why haven't you responded to my text message?" I personally think this can be tied directly to our own self-worth. Another thing that gets many people in trouble with texting is the infamous "autocorrect." Rather than run a spellcheck, we let Silicon Valley decide the correct spelling of the word we didn't want in the first place. Many an individual have gotten in trouble for not paying attention to their phone.

It's not going to be long before a smart communication device is embedded in your body so you can put your hand on your chest and say, "Beam me up, Scottie," or "Call my wife." Oh wait, we already have that with Siri or her cousin Alexa, and you don't have to put your hand on your body to send a request.

Now, take my new friends, Siri and cousin Alexa.

I asked Siri, "Where is the nearest coffee shop?"

Siri responds, "There are two coffee shops near you."

I just see the two arguing over who is correct.

Give me a break! "Siri, can you call me Bubba?"

"I do not know what a 'Bubba is. Instead, I will call you sexy."

Ok, I took some liberties with the name.

We have progressed to where we can now use Wi-Fi to communicate with the refrigerator, house lights, TV, etc …. This list goes on. I was at a large home improvement store and noticed a new refrigerator model on the sales floor that you can "knock" on the door and see what is inside. Really, can't you just open the door? Now, this is what scares me about these smart refrigerators: there are cameras inside some of these "smart" refrigerators. It's scary to think that in the middle of the night, I could open the refrigerator door, and it would respond to me by saying a line from the movie _2001: A Space Odyssey_. "Sorry Dave, I can't open the pod bay door. By the way, Dave, you need to put some clothes on." Progress, I wonder what Scottie would think when he was to beam up Capt. Kirk, and instead, there was a Millennial with their head buried in their smartphone ....

I Just Don't Understand

Throughout my life, there have been many things that I just don't understand. These things go from simplistic to complex. For example, what is the benefit of attaching your keys to a long strap that hangs down to one's knee? Now, I expect if I ask someone who has this keypad, I will probably get the response … It is "cool," oh, I mean, "kool." Or can it be that one cannot locate their keys and they need the strap to find them? This is possibly akin to the "four thousand keys" most ladies carry. Maybe I ought to ask them to describe the purpose of each key.

Next, what is it with drivers not using that little arm on the steering column called a turn signal? I used to get all frustrated with those drivers. It could be partly because I'm getting older and set in my ways … however, it dawned on me that they are doing nothing wrong … they know where they are going, and they have no need to let me know.

Ok, I can't write this without mentioning hair color. Now, I know that this is a personal preference, and I don't want to offend those who do color their hair. It's just that I don't understand ... why purple? I have some female friends that have multiple colors in their hair. When I saw them, my first sarcastic comment was, "Did you trip and fall into a bucket of paint?" This wasn't received in the manner I expected.

Now, I must explain that after I got out of the navy, the first thing I did was grow my hair long in a ponytail. It was my way of saying, "Stick this establishment where the sun doesn't shine," Since I couldn't have long hair back in the late 60s and 70s. (You know, the good boy syndrome.) It took me at least 10 years to get past this stage. Now, I'm lucky if I can keep what little hair I have left. Ugh! Since we are talking about hair, why do they call it a ponytail?

Those little ponytails or "wanna-be" should not be worn if there is not enough hair to put it in a ponytail. I can answer that because they want to be different. They could just as well call it a horsetail ... well, I can see why this wouldn't work because the horsetail is close to that part of the horse that we don't want to be associated with.

Oh, I just shake my head when I see a "man bun." Just like what a schoolteacher of the past used to wear. Why?

Next, we have the hoodie. Yeah, I know it is a "kool" thing. That said, explain this situation to me... my wife and I are sitting on the plane to come home from a trip to Cancun, Mexico. It is 88 degrees outside, passengers are loading, and then I see it. A young man, coming down the aisle, goes to his seat and has a hoodie pulled down tight around his face. This just accentuated his scraggly beard, which looked like it needed fertilizers to grow. Wait a second, didn't Shaggy from Scooby-Doo have a beard? Yep, there's the connection, Hollywood. This passenger, heading to his seat, probably has never heard of Scooby-Doo. Sorry, I got carried away. Another question I have is whether the hoodie is to cover up the individual's unwashed hair. I keep forgetting - baby boomers and the younger generation.

Have you ever seen a pair of pants halfway down one's buttocks? This can be seen in the younger generation and in some adults. No one wants to see a "worker bee" bent over and expose the crease in one's rear. All I know is my mother was constantly telling me to pull my pants up. This was followed by how I wouldn't be able to run if there was a fire or a dire emergency to use the toilet.

Speaking of pants, what is it with ripped jeans? As you know, I'm not on the younger side of life. When I was a kid, my mother would take those jeans, cut the leg portion off, and turn them into shorts. It's hard to believe that these "ripped" jeans can cost $40, $60, or even more just to look "kool."

There's that word again … "kool." It appears that it is the answer to a lot of things I just don't understand.

As I sit here having my morning coffee while catching up on the morning news, the station breaks for a commercial, which my mother would not agree to. The new commercial product is called Rinse. The actor "jabbers on" about having the time to do laundry. Really? You tell me, who wants someone else to do their dirty undergarments? Times are changing. The gap between Gen Z and boomers is getting wider and wider. Every day, there is another gimmick to get the population to buy into an easier life.

Don't get me wrong; I would have paid someone to do some tasks around the house, like painting the large great room in my house. I think I'm more focused on accomplishing those everyday tasks that we don't want to do, such as washing my drawers, grocery shopping, or cooking my food. These tasks cost money, which the younger generation has because many are still living at home. I think they call that "discretionary monies."

I'm amazed when I see a service cart full of groceries rolled out to a car and the purchased goods loaded into the car for you. Now, let me state that there are exceptions to any rule or action. Take, for example, someone who is housebound and can't get to the store to purchase the needed goods. It's just that the commercial provides the image that this is something to do to make your busy life easier. I see many things that don't make sense. Just the other day, a lady purchased a barbecue grill, which was already assembled. She didn't want to go through the hassle of putting it together and didn't want to pay for the store delivery fee. So she tried to put it in her car, and it wouldn't fit. So, I watched in amazement as she called a delivery service to pick it up and deliver it to her. Wouldn't you know it would not fit? Now, not to be deterred, she went to the customer service desk and requested that the grill be disassembled so she could get it home. The store denied her request. After much discussion, she left in a "huff" ... without the grill and a refund. Not to let an opportunity to save a dollar, I went to the service desk to see if I could purchase the grill at a discounted price. No such luck.

While having my morning coffee one day, I saw a commercial on the television for a new product for a woman's deodorant to be used all over her body. It's better than taking a bath. Once again, we strive to make life easier. Now, not to be outdone, we have a new product called "dude" wipes. Yep, that's right, a wet wipe for the man in your life ... really?

Finally, I've always wanted to learn the art of ventriloquism. I'm amazed how the comedian Jeff Dunham can handle many voices in his act. I was so impressed that my wife purchased a Little Jeff puppet. Yes, I know. The result of watching the comedy channel late at night. Anyway, the puppet came with a book on how to learn the art. After reading the instruction manual, I set out to learn this art. Now, sitting behind closed doors, I practiced the one line that had to be mastered prior to moving on to the manual. The line was as follows.

The boy bought a basketball.

Try saying this without moving your lips. I practiced and practiced, and the results were that I shouldn't quit my day job. The best I could do was ...

The doy dought a dasket dall.

Now you can see that I kept my day job. Such a frustrating exercise. By the way, the Little Jeff puppet is in his box in the garage.

I'm getting too old to try and figure out all of this. Oh, there's the doorbell with my Doordash order.

Achieved Success

I have always wanted to be one of the individuals who seek to hear wisdom and knowledge to solve problems. This was driven by those traits that I recognized early in my career, during my time as a Georgia Power Company employee.

Little did I know that my military career in the US Navy would be the main event that would shape my life as a responsible individual. My technical training was beneficial to my navy career. I joined, thinking of not having to keep from going to Vietnam. I did spend my four-year enlistment trying to make the best I could and to make my family proud. About two years into my navy career, I was given the responsibility of being the lead petty officer for the engine room. I don't really think they picked me because I was popular but rather because my last name started with the letter "U." I was told I was the Lead. Don't you just love the way the government works sometimes?

Notwithstanding my navy career, this attitude of confidence and resourcefulness was evident in my 16 years at the Georgia Power Company nuclear power plant construction and operation.

The next company that I worked for was Accenture. I was allowed to obtain my goal of becoming a consultant. This role helped me earn the reputation of taking on tasks/projects with little direction. I had to expand my goal of being a consultant to the roles of process improvement lead and project manager.

These clients included a large telecommunications company in Australia, a Chinese company in Beijing, China, and the evaluation of a computer help desk program in India.

While I was in India, the one rule was not to drink the local water. It's not as healthy as ours. You could definitely get Montezuma's revenge. I was able to survive on potatoes and scotch. After all, I was told not to drink the water.

Next was to be careful when taking the local taxis. Just as a side note, the locals thought that your manhood was at stake if you were polite and let someone in front of you. There were wide streets, as wide as four lanes. This is where it got interesting. I was told that the white center lane is merely a suggestion. They were all over the road. People honked their car horns at anything, anyone, and even cars. Whenever I took a taxi anywhere, I never looked out the front window. I would instead look out the side window. I just didn't want to see what was coming.

Of all my clients, the one that was the most challenging was the one in China. Not only did I not speak Mandarin, but adjusting to the local cuisine was a challenge. I stayed at a company-maintained apartment. This meant that I had to do my shopping and transportation, which were definitely a challenge.

When I had the chance, I would go out to one of the following restaurants. They have McDonald's - Kentucky Fried Chicken (no bones) - and, thank goodness, Starbucks. These three restaurants had menu placards on the order counter. This made it simple to order. You just point and order and hand them some Chinese money. I have no clue if that was correct or if I was supposed to get the change back. On Fridays, I tried to find a bar where I could get an adult beverage. I found out that there was a Marriott close to my apartment. I was thinking of getting myself a vodka martini. It was a tiring experience to communicate this to the bar personnel. I ended up going behind the bar and taught them how to make one. After this one session, when they would see me coming in the door, they fought over who was going to make my drink. I finally figured out that if you can do charades, you can just about exist with a foreign language. The other thing I learned was that everyone wore some type of uniform. Everybody had some type of job, whether it was an important one or not.

As I look back at my trip to China, I just couldn't believe I was in Tiananmen Square, where students led a demonstration against the government. Never in my wildest dreams would I expect to be here. There were more revelations for me. I went to the Great Wall of China and walked about a ¼ mile, taking in the history. This was truly something to behold. Next, a surprise for me was the summer palace and the Forbidden City. These two locations are where the last emperor of China lived. Finally, the tour bus stopped at the mandatory souvenir shop. You know this is typical: get something to eat and browse. I always get my wife a Christmas ornament wherever I travel. She asked that I get an ornament from China. I casually explained that China is not a Christian country, so don't expect an ornament. So here I am browsing, and all of a sudden, I see it ... a Christmas Tree. And yes, they had ornaments, just not your typical ones; they were cloisonne ornaments. These ornaments are unique and require years of craftsman training. They are made with thin copper wire and baked on enamel paint. They will remind both my wife and myself of this time in our lives.

Epilogue

It is a common understanding that life is about changes. Changes will happen, but how we embrace them is what matters. From my early life as a kid to the bravado of a teenager to my adult life, I have done all the preparation for my later life.

The US Navy was a "dose of reality" that brought things into perspective. It was not all about me but about something larger. That realization carried forth to my first job with the Georgia Power Company. However, I realized that the power company would no longer be constructing nuclear power plants after 12 years, and I had to change my future path. By leveraging my skill set, I was able to move forward toward my ultimate goal of becoming a management consultant. By leveraging my experience and a willingness to take on jobs that expanded my skill set, I earned a reputation as an individual who can be depended on to provide positive insight and solutions to problem resolution.

I think that my wife gave me the courage to continue to grow. I recognize that I learned from every negative and positive event, and they shaped me into who I am now.

About the Author

Growing up in the '60s provided a framework to discover two unique individual traits of "responsibility" and "purpose."

Moving from the typical "good kid" to living through the rebellious "teen" years to serving in the US Navy provided a better understanding of how the traits impact one's life. The US Navy provided a clear understanding of responsibility for something bigger than myself. These traits were a mainstay in my marriage to the realization that you must work at maintaining responsibility and purpose.

With my success in different industries such as government, petroleum, and telecommunications, working with companies in domestic and foreign countries in the arena of information technology, I have earned respect and a reputation for being dependable as one who could get the job done. These two traits of "Responsibility" and "Purpose" have provided guideposts throughout both common and chaotic times.

www.ingramcontent.com/pod-product-compliance
Lightning Source LLC
Chambersburg PA
CBHW061131160726
48006CB00036B/1697